Imagine a world where young children, from birth to kindergarten learn letter sounds rather than letter names. A place where babies and children sing an alphabet sound song, rather than an alphabet name song, and have the alphabet sounds ingrained by the time they enter school. Children could then string together letter sounds when ready to read, without the interruption of the letter names. Letter names, aside from long vowel names, are just mainly used in conversation when referring to a letter.

It's the letter sounds that give children something to string together to make words. Take the letter 'w' for instance. It sounds something like "double you" or "double yoo". A child may use energy wondering if the 'w' makes the 'd' 'u' 'b' 'l' 'y' or 'oo' sound and lose focus or motivation to decipher the code. At the present time children are learning to read with too much coding. The ABC song is repeated for the first 5 years of life and it doesn't actually help the child read like the sounds do.

Some children learn letter names and letter sounds, but still too much attention is on the names. Children are given the letter name, letter sound, capital letter, lowercase letter and are left wondering how to use this information to learn to read, but cannot express this to us. Some children do express it in some way, maybe by saying something like, 'no this is an 'h' like 'ayche' not a 'h' sound. Or, they may ask "why?" And they may occasionally get a good explanation of what to do, but then forget without enough consistency.

Even the letter names such as 'b' 'd' 'f' 'g' 'j' 'k' 'l' 'm' etc. don't help like the precise sounds do. If a child is trying to read a word and sees a 'b' and thinks of it's name, like 'bee' then has to rethink of the sound and wonder why it sounds like a bee, what its actual sound is, "is it a 'b' or 'ee' and why is the 'ee' there?" Then by the time the child gets back to reading the word, the child may have lost the first part of the word from short-term memory and has to start over again. We can eliminate this by using letter sounds at every opportunity: referring to letters by their sounds and leaving out the names. This will contribute to less energy wasted and more motivation. When learning to read, once a letter name is said aloud, it has caused a distraction from reading.

Letter names will still be learned. They can be learned at anytime. The alphabet song is currently everywhere! Most kids know the alphabet song by the time they enter kindergarten and sing it repeatedly. If we cut the amount of time spent on the current alphabet name song by 80% or more, children would still know it.

I encourage you to tell children early on that the 'c' makes two sounds, as well as the 'g'. This gives children the opportunity to gain familiarity with the concept early on. And once the letter names are mastered, other letter combinations should be learned, such as 'th' and 'sh', this book will help guide through the process.

In addition, the majority of reading (and writing) is done in lowercase letters. Much more time should be spent on learning lowercase letters. By my standards, 95% of the time should be spent on lowercase letters. There is a capital letter at the beginning of every sentence, and for the most part, that's it. So if a child spends most of time focusing on lowercase letters and can read everything except the first letter of every sentence the child would shortly learn the capital letters too.

There are certain letters that look so similar to many children: b, d, g, p, and q. These letters should be used in moderation in the beginning, as in this book, to allow the child to gain momentum when first learning how to read. Having too many words with these letters at once is demotivating to children. Children want to feel a sense of accomplishment. These letters a a distraction in the beginning.

This book is meant to be studied in order and reviewed regularly. Reviewing previous word groups is encouraged, but many times skipping ahead is not advised. The rules found in this book are essential for the beginning reader and should be practiced repeatedly before the introduction of new rules.

The more this book is reviewed, the stronger the neuronal pathways, the larger the connections, and the bigger the imprint of the reader's reference base.

Table of Contents

Learn the letter sounds...4
Practice distinguishing d, b, p and g...5-6
Learn the short vowel sounds..7-11
Message from the author...12-13
Short vowel sounds in 3 letter words..14-19
Short vowel sounds in 3-4 letter words..20
'ee' rule and words...21
'th' rule and words at the beginnings and ends of words..22-23
Cat in the Hat words with short vowel sounds and 'th' (3-5 letter words)..........................24
'oo' pattern and words..25
3-5 letter words in rules covered thus far...26-27
'ing' words, in words with 'ee' and 'oo' and short vowels..28-29
Learn the vowels and consonants..30
'ai' pattern and long 'ai' words 31-32
'ea' pattern and long 'ea' words..33-34
'oa' pattern and long 'oa' words..35-36
'ue' pattern and 'ue' words 37-38
Word list with 'ee' 'ai' 'ue' 'ea' 'oo' 'th' 'ing' and short vowels..39
'ch' as in chair at the beginnings and ends of words...40
Double consonants in short words..41-42
'ay' pattern and words...43
'ai' pattern presented with 'ay' words..44
Word list with 'oo' 'ue' 'ai' 'ay' 'ing' 'th' 'ee' double consonants and short vowels..............45
'ou' pattern and words...46
'igh' pattern and words..47
'er' ending and words with 'ou' 'ea' and 'ee' and short vowels.......................................48-50
Word list with 'ou' 'ee' 'ay' 'ea' 'th and ' 'oo' and short vowels.......................................51-52
'sh' words at the beginnings and ends of words with 'ee' 'ea' 'ou' short vowels and double consonants..53
Early math list with rules we have covered..54
Rarities and exceptions with 'ai' 'ea' 'ch' and 'ou'..55-59

Practice and learn all letter sounds, not letter names. Use **lowercase** letters only. The teacher and student must **ALWAYS** use a finger to point directly under the letter read. Always pronounce with the correct sound. Do not add vowels where they do not exist, for example 'b' is not 'bu', 'c' is not 'cu' etc. Try as hard as you can to isolate the the individual sound only.

Practice reading the sounds of 'd', 'b', 'g', and 'p' here and on a separate sheet of paper for several days. Practice is key, the more practice, the closer to mastery. Create a label for your student's bed, write on the label using a sharpie marker the word as such: bed. Your student will see this label every night and every morning.

d d d d d

d d d d d

d d d d d

b b b b b

b b b b b

b b b b b

p p p p p

p p p p p

p p p p p

g g g g g

g g g g g

g g g g g

Practice short vowel sounds until nearly mastered. Short 'a' is as in hat.

Short 'e' is as in 'end'.

e

Short 'i' is as in "win".

Short 'o' is as in "pot".

Short 'u' is as in "sun".

u

Throughout this book you will be presented with many words. The teacher should provide assistance reading full words as needed and help "sound out" or "think out" words by offering letter sounds, not letter names. You are encouraged to ask the student to "try again" at times before offering help, especially once the teacher is aware the student is familiar with the sound and "knows it". The teacher and student should always place the index finger under the letter for which the letter sound is being made.

The words in this book are central to this method and are among the most common in a child's vocabulary. Aside from the early math vocabulary list, children will have likely heard or used many of the words in this book.

Check out books from your local library and make it exciting when you recognize words from this book in your library books and from one book in another book. Make it exciting to find similar words with similar sounds and words that follow the same rules.

Find out how many books YOU can check-out at your local library. Different libraries have different maximums allowed. Some libraries allow an unlimited amount. I have checked-out an average of 75 books every few weeks from my local public library and all for free (both fiction and nonfiction). You can renew your books and when your student becomes attached, you can explain "we can check them out again." The more books your student is exposed to the sooner learning to read will occur. And combined with learning to read by understanding the letter patterns in words you will assure that your student has the best chance at becoming a successful reader.

You are encouraged to use positive reinforcement and compliments. Use phrases such as "good job," "wow," "excellent," "that's amazing," "you did it," "you are such a good reader," "you try and try again," "you're so smart," etc. You may also choose to offer fun activities as a response to the student's efforts such as, trips to the zoo, trips to the library, trips to the park, etc. Tell others about your student's amazing efforts and abilities while your student is listening. Make reading a part of your routine and a large part of your life.

This book contains many high-frequency words also known as sight words, which means they are the same words which reappear again and again in printed material. You will encounter words in reading materials that do not "follow the rules". These rule breakers are in the minority, and the majority follow the rules.

Some rule breakers are high-frequency words. The portion of high-frequency words that do break the rules will need to be memorized at a point when reading by understanding is established and the student can understand that there are some rule breakers that need to be memorized. Exposure to books and reading will accelerate their recognition for less labored memorization.

It is important to practice reading the words in this book regularly. Some may do it weekly. Some make practice daily. Make this book and reading books a part of your routine. Encourage your student to read SLOWLY and to read one word before moving his/her eyes and finger to the next word(s). Making flashcards for these words can give the opportunity for reading the word groups in new orders when shuffled, and isolates words thereby eliminating distraction. Use clear and standard handwriting in large dark print.

Explain that these words are 'at' ending, and let the student begin reading. Then explain that the words are 'an' ending and let the student read. Practice these words repeatedly and return again and again.

sat   hat   mat

pat   rat

ran   fan   man

pan   tan   van

Explain that the words are 'et' ending, and let the student begin reading. Then explain that the words are 'en' ending and let the student read. Practice these words repeatedly and return again and again.

pet   jet   let

met   set   wet

pen   hen   ten

Explain that the words are 'in' ending, and let the student begin reading. Then explain that the words are 'it' ending and let the student read. Practice these words repeatedly and return again and again.

pin   fin   tin

win

fit   hit   kit

lit   mit   pit

Explain that the words are 'ot' ending, and let the student begin reading. Then explain that the words are 'og' ending and let the student read. Practice these words repeatedly and return again and again.

hot   cot   got

lot   pot

fog   hog   log

Explain that the word is 'ut' ending, and let the student begin reading. Then explain that the words are 'un' ending and let the student read. Practice these words repeatedly and return again and again.

hut

fun   hun   run

sun

Let the student read and the teacher help. Practice these words repeatedly and return again and again.

sat	pet	pit
hot	hat	hun
fog	met	van
fit	pot	fan
hen	run	pin
mit	log	sun

Let the student read and the teacher help. Practice these words repeatedly and return again and again.

swim	clam	ten
trap	rat	flap
flag	run	fun
skin	spin	plop
stop	nap	frog
slip	flip	hen

Explain that when two e's are next to each other they say the letter e's name (long e). Make it fun. Let the teacher be one 'e' and the student be the other 'e' and say the long 'e' sound at the same time. Practice these words repeatedly and return again and again.

meet	feet	peek
see	sleep	sweet
beep	bee	tree
keep	feel	deer
free	green	

When the 't' and 'h' are next to each other like this, they make a 'th' sound. If the student asks why, you can say they are silly when they get together, they say their regular sounds when they're not together, but together they make a new sound. Make it fun.

Teach and practice the 'th' sounds at the beginnings and ends of these words. Let the student read. Practice these words repeatedly and return again and again.

this   that   then

thing

bath   math   moth

cloth   with

Practice these words repeatedly and return again and again. Use Dr. Seuss' *The Cat and the Hat* for practice. You can find it in almost all libraries. Read the book, then present the words and help your student read the words. Encourage your student to spot these words as you reread the book several times. Make it exciting to see these words in the book and in new books too!

plop	bump	wet
not	how	went
down	now	net
hat	bed	Thing 1
Thing 2	this	that
then		

Explain the 'oo' sound. Make the 'oo' sound together. Practice the 'oo' sound in these words. Practice these words repeatedly and return again and again.

spoon	boot	food
troop	tool	pool
broom	zoo	moon
foot	cook	hook
book	took	roof

Let the student read these words, help when needed. Practice these words repeatedly and return again and again.

flag	run	fun
skin	spin	plop
stop	nap	frog
food	bump	wet
not	how	went
down	now	net

moon   tree   spoon

green   feet   peep

Read 'ing' to your student and have the student practice reading it too. Show your student a couple of examples of "ing" ending words in a book (s)he likes.

Let the student read these words, help when needed. Offer strategy, for example, cover the 'ing' with your finger, allow the student to fully read the root word, and then remove your finger and say 'ing'. Use a fun high pitched tone. Make it fun. Practice these words repeatedly and return again and again.

sleeping   bumping

beeping   fixing

mixing   swinging

looking   seeing

Teach your student that there are vowels and consonants. Let your student memorize the vowels. There is a song from 1983 that works very well to speed this process along. It is called I.O.U. by Freeez. Sing along with your student, make it fun, dance. Encourage the y as sometimes a vowel, but there no need to emphasize it now.

Vowels:

a　　e　　i　　o　　u

y

Consonants:

b　c　d　f　g　h　j

k　l　m　n　p　q　r

s　t　v　w　x　y　z

Reread this book to this point many times, combine this with library book readings. When your student is ready, begin these long vowels sounds. Explain that when the letters 'a' and 'i' are next to each other like this: ai, we say the long 'a' sound and the 'i' is silent. The 'i' is only there to make the 'a' say 'a'. You can explain, "When [these] two vowels are walking, the first one does the talking". This is a quite common vowel pattern! Make it interesting, "When these two letters get together like this only the 'a' talks, the 'i' doesn't say anything". Compare the situation to two people who get together and one talks while the other doesn't. Move the book around the room as though it is walking. Practice now with the long 'a' sound.

See page 54 on rarities and exceptions. Note: with the majority of words with this pattern, the 'ai' has the long 'a' sound. It has the 'a' sound as in "again" in some words.

Practice these words repeatedly and return again and again.

hair	wait
paint	pail
brain	snail
rain	train
tail	stain

Explain that when the letters 'e' and 'a' are next to each other like this: ea, we say the 'e' sound and the 'a' is silent. You can explain, "When [these] two vowels are walking, the first one does the talking". This is a very common letter pattern. It makes the long 'e' sound in the majority of words, and the short 'e' sound in quite a few. It rarely makes the 'a' sound as in "great" and bear". First teach the long 'e' version as it is much more common! Move the book around the room as though it is walking. Practice now with the long 'e' sound.

See page 55 for more on rarities and exceptions.

Practice these words repeatedly and return again and again.

neat	near	hear
ear	dear	clean
heal	clear	speak
cream	leaf	meal
heat	meat	

Explain that when the letters 'o' and 'a' are next to each other like this: oa, we say the 'o' sound and the 'a' is silent. You can explain, "When [these] two vowels are walking, the first one does the talking". With the majority of words the 'oa' has the long 'o' sound. Practice now with the long 'o' sound.

Practice these words repeatedly and return again and again.

boat	goat	coat
soap	throat	road
oat	float	toad
load	roar	loaf

Explain that when the letters 'u' and 'e' are next to each other like this: ue, we say the 'u' sound as in 'blue' and the 'e' is silent. You can explain, "When [these] two vowels are walking, the first one does the talking". Practice the 'ue' sound now with the sound as in 'blue'.

Practice these words repeatedly and return again and again.

blue   true   glue

due   cue

Let the student read these words, help when needed. Practice these words repeatedly and return again and again.

drum	sing	red
swim	hand	three
pink	lungs	green
stop	train	run
flag	jump	blue
ear	sleeping	fixing
book	this	thing

Explain that when the 'c' and the 'h' are next to each other like this: ch, the 'ch' sound as in "chair" is produced. Tell the student that the letters 'ch' also makes the 'k' and 'sh' sounds, but not in as many words and that you are just focusing on the sound like 'ch' in 'chair'. Practice these words repeatedly and return again and again.

Note: the 'ch' as in "school" occurs in about less than 100 common words (a significant amount). And the 'ch' makes the 'sh' sound as in "chalet" rarely and is silent as in "yacht" very rarely.

chair	chip	chin
cheek	lunch	bench
teach	inch	

See page 65 on rarities and exceptions.
Explain that some short words have two consonants next to each other and that it's okay to just read them the same way. This happens in short words with 'dd' 'ff' 'll' 'nn' 'ss' 'tt' and 'zz'. Practice these words repeatedly and return again and again.

pass	mess	mass
kiss	miss	less
hill	will	sell
fell	fill	bell
tell	yell	inn
add	odd	mutt

mitt   jazz   buzz

puff

The majority of words containing the 'ay' pattern have the long 'a' sound. Remind the student that the 'y' is sometimes a vowel and explain that it becomes a vowel when it is at the end of a word, but is a consonant at the beginning of a word like in 'yes'. It is also so in the middle of words when a suffix is added as in "playing". The 'y' here may be considered a silent vowel as in, "When two vowels are walking the first one does the talking." If the student insists on making a consonant 'y' sound at the end of the following words, that's fine. Practice these words repeatedly and return again and again.

may	play	way
stay	spray	tray
away	day	say

Let the student read these words, help when needed. Practice these words repeatedly and return again and again.

hair	wait	paint
pail	brain	snail
rain	train	tail
stain	may	play
way	stay	spray
tray	away	day

Practice these words repeatedly and return again and again.

hot	yet	am
moon	blue	train
say	play	rain
red	hill	kiss
bump**ing**	food	spoon
bath	thing	sleep

Explain that when the letters 'o' and 'u' are next to each other like this: ou, the sound produced for most words is the 'ou' sound as in 'out'. Practice these words repeatedly and return again and again.

out	loud	shout
sound	mouth	proud
our	ouch	found
round	count	around
about		

See pages 57-58 on rarities and exceptions.

Explain that when the letters 'igh' are next to each other like this: 'igh' the sound produced is the long 'i' sound and the 'gh' are silent. Practice these words repeatedly and return again and again.

night	light
lightning	bright
might	right
slight	sight
thigh	high
sigh	

Explain that there is a word ending 'er' as in 'sticker'. Practice these words repeatedly and return again and again.

cleaner	liver
marker	rounder
teacher	letter
eater	sleeper
drinker	helper
singer	upper

bigger   jumper

after   louder

While many of the above words are high-frequency words, this is an additional list of high-frequency words, practice repeatedly and return again and again.

yet	down	out
now	feet	it
as	had	his
at	help	has
got	big	say
him	and	can

end	its	an
each	get	in
how	way	see
us	up	the
that	on	not
may	this	thing
best	let	is

did but if

just will took

away

Explain that when these two letters are next to each other like this: sh, they make the 'sh' sound as in sheep. Practice these words repeatedly and return again and again.

sheep	shop	shut
fish	leash	brush
shell	wish	dish
shout		

The following is a basic list of words frequently used in early mathematics. Learning to read math vocabulary accelerates a student's ability to read word problems, follow directions and focus on the math itself. Practice these words repeatedly.

sum	add	plus
math	count	tenth
sixth	fifth	third
inch	number	three

Rarities and exceptions:

Most words with the 'ai' pattern have the long 'a' sound as previously described. Rarely, the 'ai' has the sound as in "again". This happens when the 'ai' is in a syllable that is not stressed. This is quite a bit of information for an early reader, which is why it is best to overlook until the child is ready. The following list should be memorized at that time. Use the space below to add like words as you encounter them.

said	again	against
Britain	captain	mountain
fountain	curtain	certain
chieftain	bargain	bargained
bargaining	villain	villainy
porcelain	renaissance	

The 'ea' pattern mostly has a long 'e' sound. The 'ea' pattern has the short 'e' sound too, but less often. This is a lot of information for a young reader. Teach your student to read 'ea' using the long 'e' sound first and the following list should be memorized when your student is ready. Use the space below to add like words as you encounter them.

head	read	bread
thread	spread	lead
tread	sweat	threat
earn	yearn	learn
early	pearl	heard
search	wealth	health
dealt	real	breath
earth	breast	cleanse
meant	meadow	instead
feather	heavy	deaf

Memorize these exceptions at a later time: area, bear, beau, idea, areal, heart, nausea, break, create

The 'ch' makes the sound as in "chair" mainly. In less than 100 common words (a significant amount) it makes the sound as in "school" and rarely makes the sound as in "chalet" is is very rarely silent as in "yacht". Below is a reference for the sound as in "school". Return and memorize at a later time. Use the space below to add like words as you encounter them.

ache	scheme	school
chort	chrome	chord
choir	character	scheme
stomach	chronic	chemistry
Christmas	architect	chiropractor
monarchy	archaic	charisma
anchor	chlorine	chrysalis
chrism	echo	orchid
cholesterol	choreography	anchorite
psychology	chromium	chromosome
synchronize	Christopher	chameleon
archaeology	orchestra	zucchini
psychiatry	hierarchy	technique
scholastic	chronological	chronicle

The 'ou' makes the sounds as in "out" as previously described. But less often it makes the long 'o' sound as in "court". Here is a list for reference and memorization at a later time. Use the space below to add like words as you encounter them.

court	soul	mould
source	course	four
your	pour	mourn
dough	though	although
shoulder	courses	sources

In even less cases the 'ou' sounds like 'u' as in "you" keep this for reference and memorization at a later time. Use the space below to add like words as you encounter them.

you	youth	through
coup	group	soup
coupon	tour	wound

About the Author

Cynthia Baugh-Llerenas resides in San Diego California and is originally from Michigan. She has a master's degree from Arizona State University and a bachelor's degree from San Diego State University. Ms. Baugh-Llerenas was invited to participate in research at three neuroscience laboratories in the studies of both cognitive neuroscience and behavioral neuroscience on learning and behavior (both at San Diego State University and the University of California, San Diego).

Ms. Baugh-Llerenas, has taught English as a second language to adults at Cuyamaca College in San Diego, and she taught third-grade at Kingswood Elementary School in Surprise, AZ, where she also specialized in working with gifted children.

Contact information:
cindy.llerenas12@gmail.com
https://www.facebook.com/cynthia.llerenas.98
Phone: (858) 255-1211